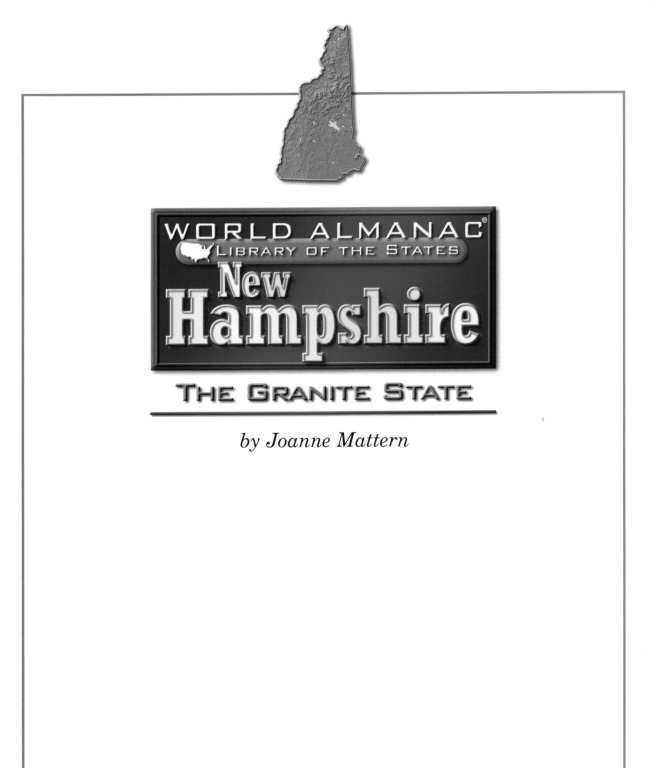

WORLD ALMANAC® LIBRARY OF THE STATES

New Hampshire

THE GRANITE STATE

by Joanne Mattern

WORLD ALMANAC® LIBRARY

Please visit our web site at: www.worldalmanaclibrary.com
For a free color catalog describing World Almanac® Library's list of high-quality books
and multimedia programs, call 1-800-848-2928 (USA) or 1-800-387-3178 (Canada).
World Almanac® Library's fax: (414) 332-3567.

Library of Congress Cataloging-in-Publication Data

Mattern, Joanne, 1963-
    New Hampshire, the Granite State / by Joanne Mattern.
        p. cm. — (World Almanac Library of the states)
    Includes bibliographical references and index.
    Contents: Almanac — History — The people — The land — Economy &
commerce — Politics & government — Culture & lifestyle — Notable people —
Time line — State events & attractions — More about New Hampshire.
    ISBN 0-8368-5155-2 (lib. bdg.)
    ISBN 0-8368-5326-1 (softcover)
    1. New Hampshire—Juvenile literature. [1. New Hampshire.] I. Title. II. Series.
F34.3.M34   2003
974.2—dc21   2002038047

First published in 2003 by
World Almanac® Library
330 West Olive Street, Suite 100
Milwaukee, WI 53212 USA

A Creative Media Applications Production
Design: Alan Barnett, Inc.
Copy editor: Laurie Lieb
Fact checker: Joan Vernero
Photo researcher: Annette Cyr
World Almanac® Library project editor: Tim Paulson
World Almanac® Library editors: Mary Dykstra, Gustav Gedatus, Jacqueline Laks Gorman,
  Lyman Lyons
World Almanac® Library art direction: Tammy Gruenewald
World Almanac® Library graphic designers: Scott M. Krall, Melissa Valuch

Photo credits: pp. 4-5 © Tom Till; p. 6 (left) © ArtToday; p.6 (right top) © ArtToday; p. 6 (right
bottom) © Tim Zurowski/CORBIS; p. 7 (top) © Positive Images; p. 7 (bottom) © Bruce Coleman;
p. 9 © Hulton Archive/Getty Images; p. 10 © North Wind Picture Archives; p. 11 © North Wind
Picture Archives; p. 12 © Hulton Archive/Getty Images; p. 13 © North Wind Picture Archives;
p. 14 © AP/Wide World Photos; p. 15 © Hulton Archive/Getty Images; p. 17 © Positive Images;
p. 18 © Linette Ellis Mathewson; p. 19 © Jack Olson; p. 20 (left) © Patricia J. Bruno/Positive
Images; p. 20 (center) © ArtToday; p. 20 (right) © ArtToday; p. 21 (left) © Positive Images; p. 21
(center) © Tom Till; p. 21 (right) © Walter Bibikow/Danita Delimont, Agent; p. 23 © Martin
Miller/Positive Images; p. 26 © Photri, Inc.; p. 27 © Walter Bibikow/Danita Delimont, Agent;
p. 29 © Bruce Coleman; p. 31 (top) © North Wind Picture Archives; p. 31 (bottom) © Hulton
Archive/Getty Images; p. 32 © Bruce Coleman; p. 33 © Positive Images; p. 34 © Linette Ellis
Mathewson; p. 35 © AP/Wide World Photos; p. 36 © AP/Wide World Photos; p. 37 (top)
© Hulton Archives/Getty Images; p. 37 (bottom) © AP/Wide World Photos; p. 38 © North Wind
Picture Archives; p. 39 © Photri, Inc.; p. 40 (top) © North Wind Picture Archives; p. 40 (bottom)
© Hulton Archive/Getty Images; p. 41 © AP/Wide World Photos; pp. 42-43 © North Wind Picture
Archives; p. 44 (top) © Positive Images; p. 44 (bottom) © Bruce Coleman; p. 45 (top) © Patricia J.
Bruno/Positive Images; p. 45 (bottom) © Bruce Coleman

Printed in the United States of America

1 2 3 4 5 6 7 8 9 07 06 05 04 03

New Hampshire

A Rugged Beauty

G ranite is a strong, rugged rock that is able to withstand harsh conditions. This rock, found throughout New Hampshire, gave the state its nickname, "The Granite State." Granite is an ideal representation of New Hampshire and its people — strong, tough, and supportive. The state of New Hampshire served as a cornerstone for the nation's future.

English settlers who began arriving in New Hampshire in the 1600s found an abundance of natural resources in the state's mountains, forests, and lakes. The state's rugged terrain and fierce winter weather, however, made life in the wilderness difficult. New Hampshire's early settlers brought with them an independent and determined spirit.

New Hampshire was one of the thirteen original colonies, and it was the first colony to break away from England. It later became the ninth state to join the United States. From its earliest days as a colony and state, New Hampshire represented freedom and independence — qualities that would later define the United States. This firm commitment to liberty gave the state its motto, "Live Free or Die." The people's determination to shape the state's laws has led to the most representational state government in the United States.

Although New Hampshire is small and often goes unnoticed in the history of the United States, it has been the home of many influential Americans. Writers such as Robert Frost and J. D. Salinger, astronaut Alan Shepard and space enthusiast Christa McAuliffe, and politicians Daniel Webster and Franklin Pierce have all shaped the nation's history and culture in important ways.

Over the years, New Hampshire has developed from a rural land of farms and forests to a prosperous place of high-tech industries and creative people. Prosperity, natural beauty, and an independent way of life have all combined to make New Hampshire a special place in the United States.

▶ Map of New Hampshire showing the interstate highway system, as well as major cities and waterways.

▼ New Hampshire's rugged landscape includes thick forests and rocky mountains.

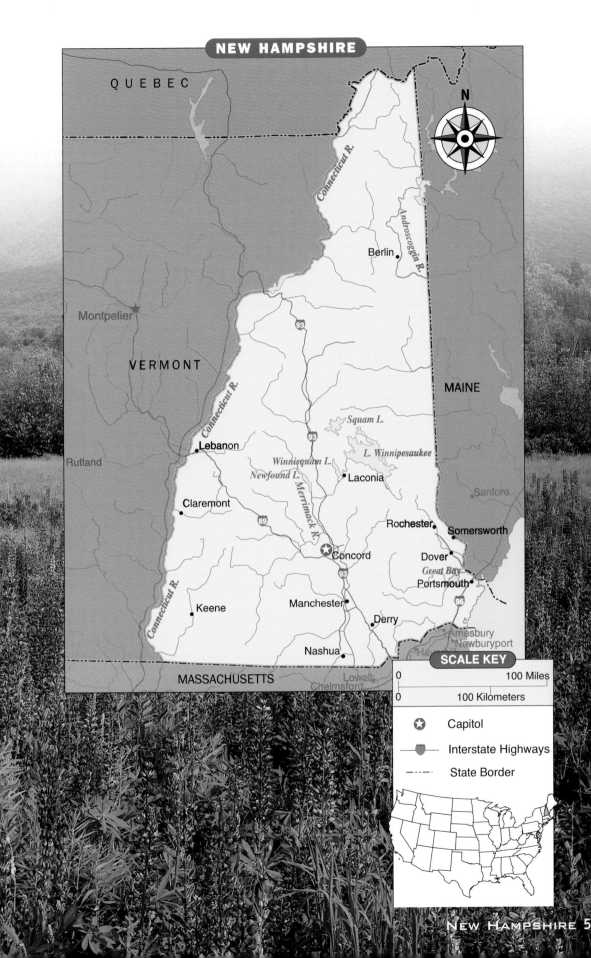

NEW HAMPSHIRE

QUEBEC

VERMONT

Montpelier

Rutland

Connecticut R.

Lebanon

Claremont

Keene

Connecticut R.

N

Berlin

Androscoggin R.

MAINE

Squam L.

L. Winnipesaukee

Winnisquam L.

Newfound L.

Laconia

Merrimack R.

Sanford

Rochester

Somersworth

Dover

Great Bay

Portsmouth

★ Concord

Manchester

Derry

Amesbury
Newburyport

Nashua

MASSACHUSETTS

Lowell
Chelmsford

SCALE KEY

0   100 Miles

0   100 Kilometers

★ Capitol

Interstate Highways

State Border

Fast Facts

New Hampshire (NH), The Granite State

Entered Union

June 21, 1788 (9th state)

Capital	Population
Concord	40,687

Total Population (2000)

1,235,786 (41st most populous state)
— *Between 1990 and 2000, the state's population increased 11.4 percent.*

Largest Cities	Population
Manchester	107,006
Nashua	86,605
Concord	40,687
Rochester	28,461
Dover	26,884

Land Area

8,968 square miles (23,227 square kilometers) (44th largest state)

State Motto

"Live Free or Die"

State Song

"Old New Hampshire" *by John F. Holmes and Maurice Hoffmann, Jr., adopted in 1949.*

State Rock

Granite — *This hard igneous rock can be found throughout New Hampshire. Its characteristics of strength and durability exemplify the ideals upon which the state was founded.*

State Insect

Ladybug — *There are about four thousand species of ladybug in the*

world. About four hundred live in the United States. Different species have different numbers of spots, ranging from none at all to about twelve.

State Wildflower

Pink lady's slipper — *The pink lady's slipper is native to New Hampshire and was named the state's official wildflower in 1991. This flower grows in moist, wooded areas.*

State Animal

White-tailed deer — *When they are startled, white-tailed deer raise their tails to reveal the white patch underneath. This signals other deer in the herd to run away.*

State Butterfly

Karner blue

State Bird

Purple finch — *Purple finches are not actually purple. Females are white and brown, and males are red and brown.*

PLACES TO VISIT

Canterbury Shaker Village, *Canterbury*

This historical village was founded by members of the Shaker religious sect and displays Shaker buildings, crafts, and furniture.

John Paul Jones House, *Portsmouth*

The Revolutionary War hero lived here briefly. Today his home features costumes, documents, and artifacts from the late 1700s.

Lake Winnipesaukee, *Laconia*

Residents and visitors enjoy many outdoor activities on New Hampshire's largest lake. It is also the site of the Wolfeboro Historical Society Museum.

For other places and events, see p. 44.

BIGGEST, BEST, AND MOST

- The Christa McAuliffe Planetarium in Concord has the most advanced planetarium projection system in the world.
- The longest covered bridge in the United States is the 460-foot (140-m) Cornish-Windsor Bridge over the Connecticut River.
- On April 12, 1934, the strongest gust of wind ever recorded on land that was not during a tornado was recorded at Mount Washington. The gust was 231 miles (372 km) an hour.

STATE FIRSTS

- **1776** On January 5, New Hampshire became the first of the thirteen colonies to declare independence from Great Britain.
- **1800** Portsmouth was chosen as the site of the U.S. Navy's first official shipyard.
- **1952** New Hampshire held the earliest presidential primary election, a tradition that continues to this day.
- **1964** New Hampshire begins the first state lottery to fund public education.

The Old Man of the Mountain

The Old Man of the Mountain is a granite formation on Profile Mountain, which is part of the White Mountains. Also known as the Great Stone Face, it looks like an old man's face peering out from the side of the mountain. Surveyors were the first people to write a description of the Old Man of the Mountain in 1805. It stands 40 feet (12 m) tall and 25 feet (8 m) wide. In 1945, it became New Hampshire's official emblem. The Old Man of the Mountain is pictured on the commemorative state quarter issued in 2000.

A Sweet Treat

Maple syrup is one of New Hampshire's most famous foods. The syrup is made from maple tree sap. During the spring, when the sap is flowing, the trees are "tapped" by inserting tubes into the trunk that allow the sap to flow into buckets. Then the sap is boiled to make a sweet, sticky syrup. Maple syrup is enjoyed by people around the world. It can be poured on pancakes, French toast, and other foods or made into a deliciously sweet candy.

A Land of Independence

> The Indians believe that every man is naturally free and independent, that no one ... on earth has any right to deprive him of his freedom and independency, and that nothing can be a compensation for the loss of it.
>
> — *From* A Concise Account of North America *by Robert Rogers, 1765*

New Hampshire's first residents arrived about ten thousand years ago. These settlers were prehistoric people who hunted bears, deer, and other large animals with stone-tipped spears. Unfortunately, little is known about these early people.

Later, Native American peoples settled along New Hampshire's coastline. By 1500 A.D., New Hampshire was home to Natives such as the Abenaki and the Pennacook. These Natives were members of the Algonquian-speaking Indian family, which once lived in most of today's eastern Canada and northeastern United States.

Abenaki and Pennacook families lived in villages of fifty to two hundred people. Their homes were dome-shaped shelters called wigwams. The people made wigwams by bending tree branches into frames, then covering them with bark. They lined the inside of each wigwam with fur to keep out the cold, wind, and snow.

The Abenaki and Pennacook were farmers and hunters. Women and children grew pumpkins, squash, beans, corn, and several different kinds of berries on small plots of land. The men fished and hunted deer, bears, foxes, and other animals. The Native Americans used the animals' meat for food and made warm clothes and blankets out of the furs and hides.

Many other Native American tribes settled in New Hampshire. They included the Nashua, Piscataqua, Coosuc, and Ossipee. By 1623, there were about five thousand Native Americans living in New Hampshire.

Native Americans of New Hampshire

Native Americans of New Hampshire
Abenaki
Coosuc
Nashua
Ossipee
Pennacook
Piscataqua

DID YOU KNOW?

Before 1600, there were more than twelve thousand Native Americans living in New Hampshire. However, wars between these people and the Mohawk, a tribe that lived to the west, killed many of New Hampshire's Native people. In addition, several epidemics spread through New England in the early 1600s, reducing the population even more.

The Europeans Arrive

The first recorded European visitor to New Hampshire was an Englishman named Martin Pring. In 1603, he sailed along the American coast from Maine to Massachusetts. In New Hampshire, Pring's ships floated up the Piscataqua River. Pring was looking for a shortcut to Asia and was not interested in settling in the area. The French explorer Samuel de Champlain also visited New Hampshire. In 1605, Champlain traveled along the New England coastline and created a map of New Hampshire. He also explored to the west, in what is now Vermont. However, Champlain had already created a settlement in eastern Canada, and he did not settle in New England.

In 1614, John Smith arrived in New Hampshire while on a whale-hunting and fur-trading expedition from England. Smith explored a great deal of New Hampshire's coast and made notes about the animals and plants that he found. He made detailed maps of the area. Although Smith did not live permanently in New Hampshire, he encouraged other English people to settle there and in other parts of New England as well.

▼ The first European settlers arrive at Odiorne's Point in 1623.

During the early 1620s, other British explorers and settlers visited the area. In 1622, King James I of England granted 6,000 acres (2,428 hectares) of land to David Thomson. Thomson and about twenty other men arrived in southeastern New Hampshire in 1623 and built a settlement called Pannaway Plantation at a place called Odiorne's Point. The settlement included a stone manor house, a smithy, a fort, and outdoor racks for drying fish. Pannaway Plantation was probably the first European settlement in New Hampshire, and Thomson's son, John, was the first child of European descent born in New Hampshire. However, the settlement lasted only a few years.

In 1622, King James also granted a large area of land to John Mason and Sir Ferdinando Gorges. In 1629, the two men divided the land. Gorges kept the northern half, which later became part of the state of Maine. Mason took the land between the Merrimack and Piscataqua Rivers. Because he was from Hampshire in England, Mason named this area New Hampshire.

By 1631, Mason had sent a group of colonists to New Hampshire. The colonists settled at a place they called Strawbery Banke, because so many wild strawberries grew

▼ Early settlers had to work hard to survive in the wilderness. Everyone in the family at Strawbery Banke helped with hunting, farming, caring for animals, and household chores.

in the area. Strawbery Banke later became Portsmouth, one of New Hampshire's most important cities.

Because of the harsh winter weather and lack of farmland, few English settlers came to New Hampshire. They preferred the warmer climate of the southern colonies. By 1640, New Hampshire had only one thousand British colonists and four settlements in the southeastern corner (Dover, Strawbery Banke, Exeter, and Hampton).

In 1641, the people of New Hampshire decided to merge with the Massachusetts Bay Colony, which was just south of New Hampshire. The relationship was rocky from the start. The people of New Hampshire disagreed with the laws and policies of the Massachusetts Bay Colony, but needed its resources to support their tiny settlements. In 1680, New Hampshire broke away, but two years later found itself under the control of Massachusetts once again. In 1692, the colony again declared independence, but remained politically bound to Massachusetts in that the two colonies shared the same governor. In 1791, the two colonies split for good, after a definite border was established. At that time, New Hampshire received its own governor.

From Colony to State

In the mid-1700s, New Hampshire grew and prospered. Heavily wooded land was cleared for farming and a seemingly unlimited supply of fish and game drew more settlers to the area.

With its excellent supply of timber and a good, deep coastline, the colony soon became a center for shipbuilding. New Hampshire's white pines were especially prized for crafting masts and the ornate figureheads of ships. Thanks to this lucrative industry, Portsmouth became an important colonial port.

New Hampshire's thriving economy attracted more settlers. But these settlers also changed the land. More timber was needed to build houses and

John Wentworth

Born in 1737, John Wentworth was a member of one of New Hampshire's most important families. His grandfather had been New Hampshire's lieutenant governor, and his uncle, Benning Wentworth, was New Hampshire's royal governor from 1741 to 1767. Although his family had connections with the British government, John Wentworth took the American side during the crisis over the Stamp Act. In 1767, Benning Wentworth was forced to resign as royal governor, and John took his place. He became popular for making improvements to New Hampshire, such as building more roads, establishing Dartmouth College, and bolstering the New Hampshire militia. Although Wentworth thought Great Britain treated the colonies "harshly and with contempt," he did not want New Hampshire to break away from Great Britain. Because of these opinions, Wentworth was forced to leave the colony. He lived in Canada until his death in 1820, but always called New Hampshire his native country.

land. More timber was needed to build houses and forts. Lakes and streams were dammed to create a water source for people to use. These changes damaged the natural environment and made it harder to find animals to hunt or fish.

Many Native Americans were angry about the changes the British brought to the area. The French, who were fighting with the British for control of the fur trade in the American colonies, encouraged the Native Americans to attack the British. This led to a series of battles called the French and Indian War. By the time the British won control of the area in 1763, many Native Americans had either died or fled to Canada.

Soon after the end of the French and Indian War, trouble began brewing between New Hampshire and Great Britain. To raise money, Great Britain had imposed new, high taxes on its colonies in America. The rebellious colonies did not think it was fair for another country far across the ocean to tell them what to do. They were

▼ Angry colonists, including those in Portsmouth, demonstrated their disdain for the Stamp Act by taking to the streets in angry protests.

THE FOLLY OF ENGLAND AND THE RUIN OF AMERICA

especially angry in 1765 when Great Britain passed the Stamp Act, which required colonists to buy tax stamps and place them on legal documents and newspapers. The people of Portsmouth were so angry about the Stamp Act that they hanged dummies representing the tax collectors from gallows and trees. Ships in the harbor flew their flags at half-mast. Protesters filled the streets, complaining about the "death of liberty."

Although the Stamp Act was repealed in 1774, New Hampshire and the other colonies continued to resent British intrusions into their lives. On December 14, 1774, about four hundred men stormed Fort William and Mary, a British fort on an island in Portsmouth Harbor. The New Hampshirites took one hundred barrels of gunpowder and some cannons and guns from the fort. (These weapons and supplies were probably used at the famous Battle of Bunker Hill in June 1775.)

The attack on Fort William and Mary was one of the first acts of war against the British government by the American colonies.

The Revolutionary War began in 1775. Although no major battles were fought in New Hampshire, the colony sent hundreds of men to join the colonial army in Massachusetts. Shipyards in Portsmouth built a number of the ships used by the Continental Navy during the war. In January 1776, New Hampshire adopted its own constitution, making New Hamshire the first colony to form a government that was separate from Great Britain.

In September 1783, the British recognized the independence of the United States at the signing of the Treaty of Paris. Then the U.S. government drew up a constitution for the former colonies to sign. On June 21, 1788, New Hampshire became the ninth state to sign the U.S. Constitution. Since nine states were required to ratify or make the document legal, New Hampshire's action effectively created the United States of America.

New Hampshire During Wartime

By 1800, New Hampshire's population had risen to 183,858. Originally, most residents had lived along the short Atlantic coastline, but more and more communities were forming in the western part of the state. To reflect this shift, the state capital was moved from Exeter to Concord in 1808.

▲ Industrial workers, such as these mill employees, drove New Hampshire's economy and provided goods to the nation during the 1800s and 1900s.

DID YOU KNOW?

The Amoskeag Manufacturing Company in Manchester was one of the world's largest textile mills in the late 1800s and early 1900s. However, the mill went bankrupt and shut down in 1936.

In 1800, eight out of ten residents were farmers. However, a new industry was about to change the face of New Hampshire and other New England states. A cotton mill was built in New Ipswich in 1804. More followed, because New Hampshire's fast-running rivers and streams were ideal sources of power for the mills' equipment.

The state became more industrial over the next sixty years. Such New Hampshire towns as Manchester, Dover, Concord, and Nashua boomed, becoming centers of industry. These towns manufactured shoes, textiles, wagons, and many other types of goods that were in demand throughout the growing country.

During the Civil War (1861–1865), New Hampshire's industrial strength helped the northern states win the war. Textile mills produced uniforms and blankets for the soldiers. Factories in Manchester produced railroad cars and engines, while the Portsmouth Naval Shipyard built warships for the northern navy. Almost forty thousand New Hampshirites fought in the Civil War, and about forty-seven hundred men died.

New Hampshire's men and women continued to contribute to war efforts during the twentieth century. More than twenty thousand men and women from the state served in World War I (1914–1918), and about sixty thousand served in World War II (1939–1945). In addition, New Hampshire's factories produced war materials, ships, and other goods to support the U.S. forces. Portsmouth's naval yard was a major producer of submarines during World War II. The naval facility employed more than 20,500 workers in 1940, up from 3,500 in 1939. Close to 1,600 New Hampshire citizens died during the war.

A Postwar Boom

New Hampshire continued to grow after World War II ended in 1945. New industries cropped up throughout southern New Hampshire to take the place of businesses that had died out after the war. Between 1951 and 1955,

▲ The Seabrook Nuclear Power Plant has been controversial throughout its history. The plant generates 7 percent of New England's electricity.

New Hampshire and the World

In 1905, President Theodore Roosevelt helped negotiate a treaty that ended the Russo-Japanese War. The treaty, signed in Portsmouth, became known as the Treaty of Portsmouth. Roosevelt was awarded the 1906 Nobel Peace Prize for his work. In 1944, when representatives of forty-four countries met at Bretton Woods in the White Mountains, they discussed ways to pay for wartime damage and created the International Monetary Fund and the World Bank. Because of its location, the meeting became known as the Bretton Woods Conference.

almost 1,000 new businesses found homes in New Hampshire. The manufacture of electronics, tools, and paper led the postwar surge. Many industries located in the southern part of the state due to its favorable location near Boston, a large city in Massachusetts. The availability of jobs drew many new families to the region. Northern New Hampshire remained rural, however, as the population of the state doubled between 1960 and 1988 to 1.1 million people.

New industries also brought problems to the state. Many residents protested against the building of a nuclear power plant in Seabrook during the late 1970s. They argued that the plant was dangerous and would damage New Hampshire's environment. However, they eventually lost the fight. Seabrook opened in 1990 and has cut New Hampshire's reliance on oil by 30 percent.

Today, New Hampshire is a prosperous state, with many industries and jobs. As has been true throughout its history, New Hampshire is a place where independence and hard work are cherished, and people stand together to support their high standards and beliefs.

Christa McAuliffe

On January 28, 1986, the nation's attention was captured by a very special space shuttle launch. For the first time, an ordinary citizen would travel into space. This citizen was Sharon Christa McAuliffe, a social studies teacher at Concord High School who had been chosen for the journey from among eleven thousand teachers. Although she was born in Massachusetts in 1948, McAuliffe had lived and taught in Concord for eight years. She was excited about bringing her unique view of space travel to the world and planned to teach several lessons from space. Tragically, McAuliffe's dreams did not come true. Just over a minute after liftoff, the space shuttle *Challenger* exploded, killing all seven on board. Concord has not forgotten McAuliffe. The city is home to the Christa McAuliffe Planetarium, a state-of-the-art science museum dedicated to teaching children and adults about the wonders of space.

Left: Christa McAuliffe, who died in the *Challenger* explosion, was an outstanding teacher who gave her life to science.

Making Their Way

> I'm proud to be a resident of a state that best exemplifies so many of the legendary characteristics of the mystical New Englander, even those not always considered by some to be attractive. I'm speaking of frugality, fierce independence, shrewd business sense, ingenuity — and not a little pride.
>
> — *Judson D. Hale, Sr., editor-in-chief of* Yankee *magazine*

New Hampshire is a small state, but it is growing rapidly. Between 1990 and 2000, the state's population increased by 11.4 percent. This was the fastest rate of growth north of Delaware. Still, the entire state of New Hampshire has only about as many people as many large cities in other states.

Most of New Hampshire's people live in the southern part of the state. Half of the state's residents live in cities, such as Manchester, Portsmouth, Dover, Concord, and Nashua. However, these cities are small compared to other cities around the nation.

Concord, which has more than forty thousand residents, is New Hampshire's capital city. The city is home to many historical buildings, such as the State House and the Pierce

Age Distribution in New Hampshire
(2000 Census)

Age	Population
0–4	75,685
5–19	268,480
20–24	68,766
25–44	381,240
45–64	293,645
65 & over	147,970

Patterns of Immigration

The total number of people who immigrated to New Hampshire in 1998 was 1,010. Of that number, the largest immigrant groups were from India (9%), China (7.2%), and Canada (5.7%).

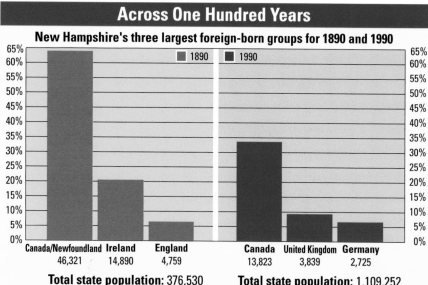

Across One Hundred Years

New Hampshire's three largest foreign-born groups for 1890 and 1990

1890 | 1990

Canada/Newfoundland	Ireland	England
46,321	14,890	4,759

Canada	United Kingdom	Germany
13,823	3,839	2,725

Total state population: 376,530
Total foreign-born: 72,340 (19.2%)

Total state population: 1,109,252
Total foreign-born: 41,193 (3.7%)

Manse, which was once the home of President Franklin Pierce. The city also includes an arts center, many museums, the Christa McAuliffe Planetarium, and several shopping districts.

New Hampshire has a high quality of life. The state has one of the lowest violent crime rates in the United States, as well as one of the lowest poverty rates. In 1997, *Money* magazine rated Nashua as the best place to live in the United States. Manchester and Portsmouth were listed in the top ten.

▲ Every September, the New Hampshire Highland Games celebrate Scottish culture.

Ethnicities

During the nineteenth and early twentieth centuries, people from Canada, Ireland, Poland, Portugal, Greece, and other countries came to New Hampshire looking for work and a better life. New Hampshire today is an ethnically homogeneous state, with 96 percent of its population being white. Almost two percent of residents call themselves Hispanic, and just over one percent are Asian. Fewer than one percent are African American or Native American.

The largest ethnic group in New Hampshire consists of French Canadians. Most live close to the Canadian border.

Over the past few years, many high-tech industries have

DID YOU KNOW?

In 1899, the Pierce Manse, threatened with demolition, was purchased by an organization called The Pierce Brigade. In 1971, The Pierce Brigade moved the house to its present site in Concord's historical district.

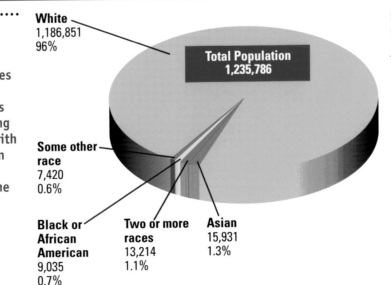

Heritage and Background, New Hampshire — Year 2000

▶ Here is a look at the racial backgrounds of New Hampshirites today. New Hampshire ranks forty-fifth among all U.S. states with regard to African Americans as a percentage of the population.

American Indian and Alaska Native
2,694
0.2%

Some other race
7,420
0.6%

Black or African American
9,035
0.7%

Two or more races
13,214
1.1%

Asian
15,931
1.3%

White
1,186,851
96%

Total Population
1,235,786

Note: 1.7% (20,489) of the population identify themselves as **Hispanic** or **Latino,** a cultural designation that crosses racial lines. Hispanics and Latinos are counted in this category as well as the racial category of their choice.

come to the state. These new industries have led to an increase in the number of Asian immigrants — men and women well educated by their countries' early advances in technology. Indians and Koreans make up most of these Asian immigrants. However, New Hampshire's population remains overwhelmingly white, and most of its immigrants still come from Canada and western Europe.

Religion

For much of its history, most people in New Hampshire belonged to Protestant groups. At one time, every town had a Congregationalist church. Members of other major sects included Anglicans, Baptists, and Quakers. These religions reflect the backgrounds of the British immigrants who originally settled New Hampshire.

Educational Levels of New Hampshire Workers (age 25 and over)	
Less than 9th grade	32,426
9th to 12th grade, no diploma	71,328
High school graduate, including equivalency	247,723
Some college, no degree or associate degree	236,406
Bachelor's degree	153,874
Graduate or professional degree	82,230

▼ The skyline of Manchester, New Hampshire's largest city.

Almost all of the French Canadians who settled in New Hampshire were Roman Catholic. Today, approximately one-third of New Hampshirites are Roman Catholic, making it the predominant religious group in the state. New Hampshire also has a small population of other religious denominations, including Judaism, Islam, and Greek Orthodox.

Education

New Hampshire established public education as early as 1647, when the colony was still part of Massachusetts. Until 1919, each town or district supervised its own schools. Since then, public schools have been controlled by a state board of education. The seven members of the board are appointed to five-year terms by the governor.

▲ Many New Hampshire towns still have old-fashioned Protestant churches, such as this one.

During New Hampshire's early days, children went to school in one-room schoolhouses. Today, New Hampshire's children attend modern schools, just like most children throughout the United States. New Hampshire was the site of the first public high school in the nation, founded in Portsmouth in 1830. New Hampshire also had the first free public library, which opened in Peterborough in 1833.

New Hampshire's public schools are supported by property taxes. This has led to inequalities in the school districts, since large, wealthy towns have more money to spend on schools than small, rural areas. To increase funding for all public schools in the state, New Hampshire began the first state lottery to fund public education in 1964. In 2001, the lottery generated more than $59 million for schools.

New Hampshire's students are considered some of the best educated in the country. The state has more than two hundred thousand students enrolled in more than five hundred public schools and about 150 non-public schools. The state's high school students have the highest graduation rate in New England; 85 percent of New Hampshire's adults have graduated from high school.

New Hampshire has approximately thirty colleges and other schools of higher education. The oldest and most famous is Dartmouth College in Hanover, which was founded in 1769 by Reverend Eleazer Wheelock. Today, it is considered one of the best colleges in the nation.

Enjoying History

New Hampshire's people take their history seriously, but they like to have fun with it too. Many New Hampshirites celebrate history by re-enacting important events, such as battles from the French and Indian War. "Living history" villages show visitors how people lived and worked in the past, while county fairs include old-fashioned activities like vegetable and livestock contests and traditional children's games.

Nature's Majesties

> You do not know New Hampshire unless you are familiar with its back roads which wind through valleys of smaller streams or climb the steep pitch of a hill here or there. They cut through pastures where great rocks crop out from between juniper and sweet fern. Miles of stone wall interlace the surrounding countryside and an occasional weather-beaten sugar house stands half hidden among the maples.
>
> — *From* Let Me Show You New Hampshire
> *by Ella Shannon Bowles, 1938*

New Hampshire may be one of the smallest states, but it includes some of the nation's most breathtaking scenery. These natural features were shaped by glaciers pushing through the area millions of years ago. From the rugged mountains to the thick forests, from lakes to ocean coastline, from farmland to protected wetlands, the state is home to an astonishing range of natural wonders.

The Coastal Lowlands

Although most of New Hampshire is hilly, there is an area of low-lying, flat land in the southeastern corner of the state. This coastal region borders the Atlantic Ocean. New Hampshire has a short coastline — only 18 miles (29 km) long.

Most of New Hampshire's coastline is made of sandy beaches. In some places, the ocean extends inward in long fingers called estuaries. Estuaries, which contain both fresh

Highest Point
Mount Washington
6,288 feet (1,917 m) above sea level

▼ *From left to right:* **Pierce Manse, the home of Franklin Pierce; White Mountain backpackers; lilacs in bloom; a white-tailed deer; a covered bridge spanning the Ammonoosus River; sailboats on Lake Winnepesaukee.**

water and salt water, are home to a variety of birds, fish, and other animals.

Portsmouth, the state's only major shipping port, is located in the Coastal Lowlands. A few miles off Portsmouth's shore are nine islands called the Isles of Shoals. Four of the islands belong to New Hampshire, and the other five belong to Maine. Few people live on these rocky islands, although the population increases seasonally.

New England Upland

The New England Upland covers all of southern New Hampshire except for the Coastal Lowlands area. The Upland is an area filled with lakes, forests, and gently rolling hills. Much of the state's granite is mined from the New England Upland near the city of Concord.

Three of New Hampshire's largest cities are located in the New England Upland. These cities — Manchester, Concord, and Nashua — are in the Merrimack River Valley, which runs through the south-central part of the state. Although much of this region has become crowded with homes and industries, there are several protected natural areas where visitors can walk through wetlands, forests, and open fields. The Connecticut River forms much of New Hampshire's western border.

New Hampshire's largest lake, Lake Winnipesaukee, is located north of the Merrimack River. This area, known as the Lakes Region, includes 273 lakes. The Lakes Region has become a popular destination for tourists in the summer. Here, visitors can enjoy swimming, fishing, canoeing, and other water sports.

Although most of the New England Upland is made of hills and fields, there is one mountain in the area. Mount Monadnock is located in the southwestern corner of the state. At 3,165 feet (965 m), it is the tallest mountain in the

Average January temperature
Manchester: 19°F (-7.2°C)
Lancaster: 14°F (-10°C)

Average July temperature
Manchester: 70°F (21.1°C)
Lancaster: 66°F (18.8°C)

Average yearly rainfall
Manchester: 39 inches (99.1 cm)
Lancaster: 37 inches (94 cm)

Average yearly snowfall
Manchester: 60.6 inches (153.9 cm)
Lancaster: 72 inches (182.9 cm)

Largest Lakes
Lake Winnipesaukee 44,586 acres (18,044 hectares)
Squam Lake 6,765 acres (2,738 ha)
Lake Winnisquam 4,264 acres (1,726 ha)

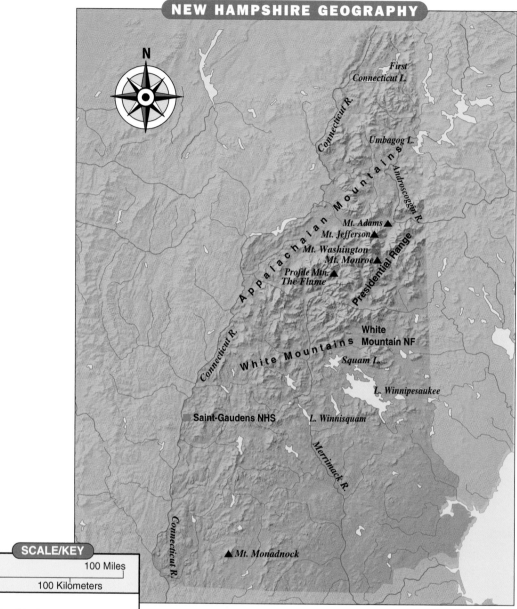

First
Connecticut L.

Connecticut R.

Umbagog L.

Androscoggin R.

Appalachian Mountains

Mt. Adams ▲
Mt. Jefferson ▲
Mt. Washington
Mt. Monroe ▲

Presidential Range

Profile Mtn.; ▲
The Flume

White Mountains

White
Mountain NF

Connecticut R.

Squam L.

L. Winnipesaukee

Saint-Gaudens NHS

L. Winnisquam

Merrimack R.

Connecticut R.

▲ Mt. Monadnock

SCALE/KEY

0	100 Miles
0	100 Kilometers

NF	National Forest
NHS	National Historical Site
▲	Highest Point
▲	Important Peaks
▓	Mountains

area. Mount Monadnock was formed when glaciers swept through the area and wore away the land around it.

The White Mountains

The White Mountains region is made up of the White Mountains in the central part of the state and all the land north to the Canadian border. The White Mountains probably got their name from their white, snow-capped peaks. They are part of the Appalachian Mountains, which stretch from Maine all the way to Georgia.

Part of the White Mountains is known as the Presidential Range. The range includes peaks named after presidents. The tallest of these is Mount Washington, which is the highest mountain in New Hampshire. Other presidential peaks include Mounts Jefferson, Monroe, and Adams. Each mountain measures more than 5,300 feet (1,615.4 m) in height.

Profile Mountain is also found in the White Mountains. This mountain is famous for a granite formation near its peak — known as the Old Man of the Mountain — that is shaped like a person's profile.

The White Mountains are located in a heavily forested area that includes more than one hundred waterfalls, brooks, and streams. The Flume is an 800-foot (244 m) granite canyon filled with rushing water and hidden caves, located in the White Mountain National Forest.

The far northern part of New Hampshire is often called "the North Country" or "the Great North Woods." This area begins north of the White Mountains and stretches all the way to the border of the Canadian province of Quebec. Few people live in this remote area. It has many fir, hemlock, maple, and birch forests. Timber companies own much of the land. People fish for smallmouth bass in Lake Umbagog, along the Maine border, and for rainbow trout and salmon in the Connecticut Lakes. The North Country is also filled with wild animals. It is not unusual to see bears, moose, and other animals walking along the side of the road.

Major Rivers
Connecticut River 407 miles (655 km)
Androscoggin River 177 miles (285 km)
Merrimack River 116 miles (187 km)

DID YOU KNOW?

The town of Clarksville, in northern New Hampshire, was built on the Forty-fifth Parallel — the halfway point between the equator and the North Pole.

▼ Franconia Notch is a passageway through the White Mountains.

Tourism and Factories

> [Visitors] may go to Vermont for repose, but they come to New Hampshire for inspiration.
> — *Jim McIntosh, travel writer*

Until the late 1800s, New Hampshire's economy depended almost entirely on agriculture, lumber, and mining. Early settlers grew vegetables and fruit and raised cattle for dairy and beef products. New Hampshire's thick forests provided lumber for building projects around the nation. The state's granite was used to build such famous buildings as the Library of Congress in Washington, D.C., and the United Nations headquarters in New York City.

The arrival of factories and mills in the late 1800s changed the state's economy to rely more on manufacturing. Factories were built along New Hampshire's waterways to harness the water's power to run machinery. Textile mills were the most common industry, providing jobs for thousands of immigrants from Canada and Europe.

Although the state suffered through an economic depression during the 1930s, as did the rest of the nation, things began to change during World War II. New Hampshire's factories produced materials for the war effort. Later, the state became home to many companies specializing in electronics and technology.

Agriculture, Forestry, and Mining

Although agriculture, forestry, and mining were once important industries in New Hampshire, they are a very small part of the state's economy today. Most of New Hampshire's farms are small family businesses. Hay and vegetables are the chief crops, along with apples, strawberries, and raspberries. The Connecticut River Valley is home to most of the state's dairy farms and animals are also raised for beef and eggs.

Top Employers
(of workers age sixteen and over)

Services	40.0%
Wholesale and retail trade	17.3%
Manufacturing	18.1%
Transportation, communications, and other public utilities	6.8%
Construction	6.8%
Finance, insurance, and real estate	6.3%
Federal, state, and local government (including military)	3.8%
Agriculture, forestry, fisheries, and mining	0.9%

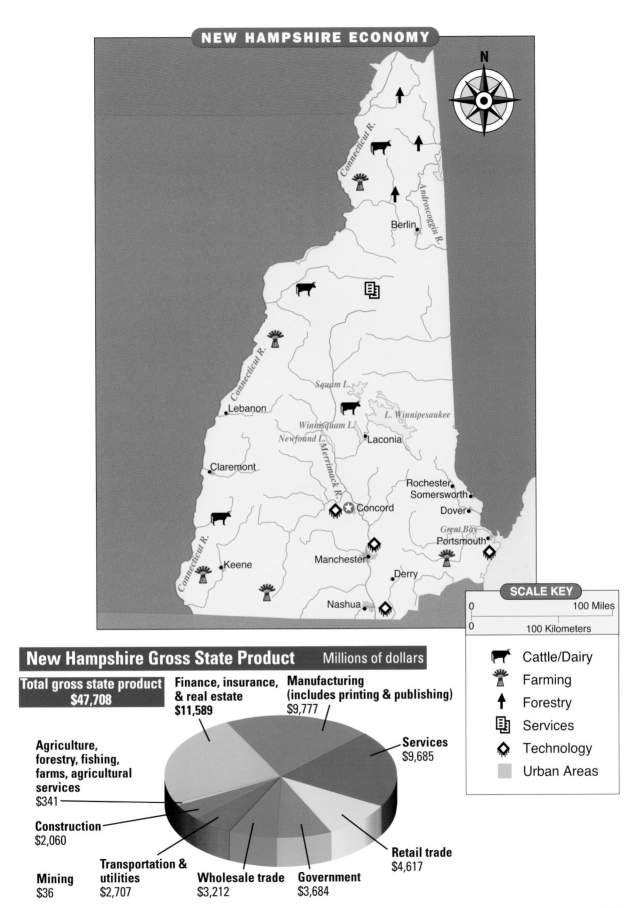

NEW HAMPSHIRE ECONOMY

Connecticut R.
Androscoggin R.
Berlin
Connecticut R.
Squam L.
L. Winnipesaukee
Lebanon
Winnisquam L.
Newfound L.
Laconia
Merrimack R.
Claremont
Rochester
Somersworth
Concord
Dover
Great Bay
Portsmouth
Manchester
Keene
Derry
Nashua
Connecticut R.

SCALE KEY

0   100 Miles
0   100 Kilometers

- Cattle/Dairy
- Farming
- Forestry
- Services
- Technology
- Urban Areas

New Hampshire Gross State Product — Millions of dollars

Total gross state product $47,708

Finance, insurance, & real estate $11,589

Manufacturing (includes printing & publishing) $9,777

Services $9,685

Agriculture, forestry, fishing, farms, agricultural services $341

Construction $2,060

Mining $36

Transportation & utilities $2,707

Wholesale trade $3,212

Government $3,684

Retail trade $4,617

More than one hundred logging companies operate in New Hampshire. These companies own most of the forests in the far northern part of the state. Forests in other areas of the state are protected by law and cannot be cut down.

Although New Hampshire once produced a large amount of the nation's granite, the mining industry is now extremely small. Today, New Hampshire's major mining products are sand, gravel, and crushed stone used to build roads.

Manufacturing

Manufacturing has been one of New Hampshire's major industries since the rise of the textile mills in the late 1800s. The textile mills, shoe factories, and other industries of that period gradually went out of business during the 1930s and 1940s. After World War II, a new type of manufacturing came to New Hampshire. The Merrimack River Valley is now home to most of the state's newer industries, which produce computers, aircraft parts, medical and scientific equipment, and other high-technology products. Many industries have come to New Hampshire because the state has no income or sales tax, which makes it more economical for companies to operate there.

Life in the Mills

In the late 1800s, the largest mill in New Hampshire could produce four million yards of fabric a week. Work in the mill was difficult for the thousands of employees who spent their days surrounded by deafening weaving looms and

Changing Needs

During the early part of its history, New Hampshire's forests provided the masts for British navy warships and New England clipper ships. Later, the wood was used to build Concord stagecoaches, which carried settlers west to the frontier. These demands made lumber an important part of New Hampshire's economy. Today, New Hampshire's trees are still important, but they are used for a different purpose. Most of the timber is used to manufacture pulp and paper products.

dirty, dusty air. The textile industry in New Hampshire today is just a fraction of what it once was. More efficient machinery requiring fewer "hands" to do the job was installed, and the demand for product subsided in the postwar years. The mills are no longer a major source of income for New Hampshire. During the twentieth century, cloth factories in the South produced materials for a lower cost. Production now has shifted to other parts of the world where labor is less expensive.

▲ The Mount Washington Hotel is one of the most luxurious hotels in New Hampshire. Every year, tourists on vacation stay in the state's hotels, providing an important source of income.

Services and Tourism

Today, most of New Hampshire's workers are in the service industry. They include employees in stores and restaurants, teachers, doctors, and those who work in communications.

Tourism has been an important part of New Hampshire's economy for more than one hundred years. Travelers in the late nineteenth century came to the state to enjoy New Hampshire's peaceful settings and natural beauty. Many wealthy families had summer homes in New Hampshire, while others stayed in scenic hotels or resorts. During the 1930s, skiers discovered the state.

New Hampshire's government responded to the increased number of tourists by building better highways and expanding public parks and camping facilities. Currently, thousands of visitors come to New Hampshire each year to enjoy its rugged splendor. These visitors hike and camp in the woods, ski in the White Mountains, sail on the lakes, fish in the ocean, and admire the beautiful colors of the leaves during the fall. Tourists spend more than $1 billion in New Hampshire every year, creating numerous jobs for restaurant and hotel workers, guides, museum staff, and workers in stores and souvenir stands that cater to visitors.

Major Airports		
Airport	Location	Passengers per year (2000)
Manchester Airport	Manchester	3,169,301

Made in New Hampshire

Leading farm products and crops
Dairy products
Nursery and greenhouse products
Hay
Vegetables
Fruit
Maple syrup and sugar products

Other products
Machinery
Electrical and electronic products
Plastics
Fabricated metal products

An Independent Spirit

> We believe we're one of the last places where, without spending a fortune, you can establish yourself as a viable candidate for President of the United States.
>
> — *Donna Sytek, speaker of the New Hampshire house of representatives, 1996–2000*

New Hampshirites are fiercely independent and determined to run their state government in the spirit of cooperation and inclusion. New Hampshire has more members in its house of representatives than any other state. Residents want their voices to be heard.

New Hampshire's constitution, ratified in 1784, is the oldest in the United States. The constitution today is very similar to the original version written more than two hundred years ago. However, every seven years, New Hampshire's voters have a chance to change, or amend, the constitution. These amendments must be passed by two-thirds of the voters.

Like the federal government and the governments of other states, New Hampshire's government is divided into three branches: executive, legislative, and judicial. The executive branch administers laws, the legislative branch makes laws, and the judicial branch interprets laws.

The Executive Branch

New Hampshire's governor is the state's chief executive officer. The governor appoints state officials, prepares the budget, and makes recommendations to the state legislature. The governor can also call up the state's military in case of an emergency.

The governor appoints several major officials including state attorney general. Unlike some other states, New Hampshire has no lieutenant governor. Instead, a five-member council, called the executive council or governor's council, assists the governor. Each member represents a different area of New Hampshire. Because different parts of the state have

State Constitution

"The people of this state have the sole and exclusive right of governing themselves as a free, sovereign, and independent state; and do, and forever hereafter shall, exercise and enjoy every power, jurisdiction, and right, pertaining thereto, which is not, or may not hereafter be, by them expressly delegated to the United States of America in congress assembled."

— *Article 7 of the New Hampshire Constitution*

Elected Posts in the Executive Branch		
Office	Length of Term	Term Limits
Governor	2 years	None
Executive Council	2 years	None

different needs, this arrangement insures that the governor will hear from all of his or her constituents and understand what is important to them. The council also approves the governor's appointments and gives advice on public matters.

The Legislative Branch

New Hampshire's state legislature is called the general court. It is divided into two sections. The house of representatives has four hundred members, which makes it one of the largest legislative bodies in the English-speaking world. The senate has twenty-four members. Members of both the house and the senate write and pass New Hampshire's laws. Each legislator serves a two-year term.

The Judicial Branch

The state supreme court is the highest court in New Hampshire. The supreme court includes a chief justice and four associate justices. These judges are the final word on law and court cases in the state. They decide if lower courts are doing their jobs properly and

▼ The Capitol Building in Concord was built in 1819. Visitors can tour the grounds, which include statues of many famous New Hampshire residents, as well as the room where the legislature meets.

interpreting the law correctly. The supreme court also evaluates whether a law or legal decision goes against the state constitution.

There are three other levels of courts under the supreme court: superior court, district courts, and probate court. All judges are appointed by the governor and the executive council. They can serve until they reach the age of seventy, retire, or are removed for good cause.

Local Government

New Hampshire has 10 counties and 221 towns. Each of these towns has its own government. Elected town leaders, whether they are male or female, are called selectmen. They are responsible for maintaining roads, providing police coverage, and delivering services to residents of that town.

Every town holds a town meeting once a year. There, every citizen who is eighteen years old or older can speak out on public issues, on which the selectmen then vote. Topics such as new laws, town improvements, and local elections are decided. Town meetings provide a chance for all adult citizens to make their voices heard in New Hampshire's government.

National Representation

Like all states, New Hampshire has two senators in the U.S. Senate. New Hampshire also has two representatives in the U.S. House of Representatives, where representation is based on population. This number has not changed since the last midterm election in 2002. In the 2004 presidential election, New Hampshire will have four Electoral College votes, just as it had in the 2000 election.

New Hampshire Politics

Until 1850, New Hampshire voted Democratic on the local, state, and national levels. However, between 1850 and the 1960s, the state's population became more conservative and shifted support to the Republican Party. Since the 1970s, the state has become more politically balanced and Democrats occupy many state offices.

General Court			
House	Number of Members	Length of Term	Term Limits
Senate	24 senators	2 years	None
House of Representatives	400 representatives	2 years	None

FRANKLIN PIERCE (1853–1857)

Franklin Pierce was born in a log cabin in Hillsboro in 1804. (His father served two terms as governor of New Hampshire.) Pierce studied at Bowdoin College and later served as brigadier general in the Mexican War. Returning home, he served in the state legislature, U.S. House of Representatives, and U.S. Senate. In 1852, the Democratic Party chose Pierce as a compromise candidate. He went on to win the election. At the time, he was the youngest man ever elected president. During his one term of office, Pierce convinced the Japanese to open their ports to the rest of the world and also acquired land from Mexico, known as the Gadsden Purchase. He supported the right of each state to individually decide whether or not to outlaw slavery, a position that probably cost him the presidential nomination in 1856. Pierce spent the rest of his life in New Hampshire, where he died in 1869.

Although it is a small state, New Hampshire has a big impact on national politics. Each election year since 1952, New Hampshire has held the first presidential primary in the nation. The New Hampshire primary is usually held in February, nine months before Election Day. This allows presidential hopefuls to test their candidacy and make themselves known before a national audience. Often, the person who becomes president of the United States is the same person who won the New Hampshire primary.

Taxes are an important political issue in New Hampshire, one of the few states that does not have an income tax or sales tax, although this means higher property taxes and other taxes. Throughout the 1990s, the state's governors have been elected based on their opposition to taxes. In 1999, the state legislature voted to add a new property tax to fund education so that all children in the state would receive a good education regardless of where they lived.

In 1996, New Hampshire residents elected state senator Jeanne Shaheen as the state's first female governor. She was reelected in 1998 and 2000. Shaheen was also the first Democrat to hold the office since 1982.

▼ Presidential candidate Al Gore (right) debated fellow candidate Bill Bradley at Dartmouth College in 1999. Like other presidential candidates, Gore and Bradley knew that winning the New Hampshire primary would be an important step toward the White House.

The Good Life

> **This is the second greatest show on earth.**
> — *P. T. Barnum, who said his own circus was "the greatest show on earth," while admiring the view from Mount Washington, date unknown*

No matter what your interests are, odds are that you will find something to suit your tastes in New Hampshire. The state is rich in history, and many areas bring the past to life in entertaining ways.

The harbor city of Portsmouth has many cobblestone streets and buildings dating from the 1700s and 1800s. Many of these buildings are now museums or historic sites that can be toured for a glimpse of life in the past. Strawbery Banke Museum is a historic district of forty-two buildings and several gardens near the waterfront. This museum recreates life in the area as it was during the 1700s. Visitors can also tour fishing boats in Portsmouth harbor and book passage on a whale-watching trip or other cruise.

Visitors to Manchester can tour the old mills that once made the city one of the industrial centers of New England. Today, many of these mills have been turned into modern office buildings.

Wakefield, in the Lakes Region of New Hampshire, also has a thriving historic district. The Museum of Childhood shows visitors how children lived and played during the early years of the nation's birth. Near the town center is Wakefield Corner, an area that includes houses built more than two hundred years ago.

DID YOU KNOW?

The Shakers, a religious group, are credited with designing useful products of superior quality including furniture and household tools. Shaker Village in Canterbury is a museum where visitors can see their handiwork.

▼ Portsmouth, one of the oldest cities in the United States, still has a thriving waterfront community.

New Hampshire's capital, Concord, is the home of the historic State House and the New Hampshire Historical Society. You can also visit the Pierce Manse, home of Franklin Pierce, and see his grave in the Old North Cemetery. Just north of Concord is Canterbury, with its Shaker Village — a historic site dedicated to the Shaker community that once called Canterbury home.

New Hampshire also has many lakes, parks, and forests. Thousands visit Lake Winnipesaukee, New Hampshire's largest lake, every year, where they enjoy swimming, boating, fishing, and camping. Nearby Weirs Beach features an old-fashioned boardwalk and boat trips on the lake. Another lakeside town is Wolfeboro, which includes Wentworth State Beach. Wolfeboro also features a scenic walking path across the Russell C. Chase Bridge that passes several tumbling waterfalls.

The largest parkland in New Hampshire is the White Mountain National Forest, in the north-central part of the state. About six million visitors come to this forest every year to hike, fish, picnic, ski, camp, and ride snowmobiles. The forest includes many campgrounds as well as some 1,200 miles (1,931 km) of hiking trails and 650 miles (1,046 km) of fishing streams.

▲ New Hampshire's White Mountains are full of opportunities for outdoor fun.

Covered Bridges

More than sixty covered bridges in New Hampshire are still in use today. Originally, bridges were covered to protect them from the heavy snows and rough winter weather. The first covered bridges, built in the 1800s, had an opening that was large enough to fit a wagon carrying a load of hay. Covered bridges were also called "kissing bridges," because so many young couples went inside them to kiss in private.

Elsewhere in the state are other wilderness areas for hikers and campers. The most popular is Mount Monadnock, which has been called the most-climbed peak in the United States. The mountain is a fairly easy climb with a breathtaking view of hills, forests, and farmlands. The view is especially beautiful during the fall, when the leaves are changing color.

New Hampshirites and visitors alike enjoy the New Hampshire Heritage Trail, a hiking path that extends for 230 miles (370 km) from the Canadian border south to Nashua. They also enjoy biking and climbing through the Polar Caves in the Baker River Valley near Plymouth. In winter, New Hampshire's mountains provide excellent skiing and snowboarding.

Libraries and Museums

New Hampshire has many museums that cover a range of different topics. The Museum of New Hampshire History is located across the street from the State House in Concord. Its many exhibits describe the history of the state and its products, from Native American times to the more recent past.

▲ Visitors to Concord's Museum of New Hampshire History can learn how people lived hundreds of years ago.

DID YOU KNOW?

The Museum of New Hampshire History features an exhibit of Concord Coaches, which were sturdy carriages used throughout the West during the 1800s. The coaches were made in Concord beginning in 1827.

The Tuck Memorial Museum in Hampton includes a one-room schoolhouse, an early fire station, farm equipment, and toys and tools from hundreds of years ago.

For a more modern perspective, you can visit the Wright Museum in Wolfeboro, dedicated to life in the United States during World War II. On exhibit are many artifacts from the period, including uniforms, weapons, clothing, vehicles, and films.

New Hampshire's leading art museum is the Currier Gallery of Art in Manchester. It contains artwork from all over New England, silver, pewter, furniture, and one of the largest collections of glass paperweights in the world.

Smaller museums throughout the state honor famous New Hampshirites. Robert Frost's home in Derry, Daniel Webster's birthplace in Franklin, and the John Paul Jones House in Portsmouth are all open to the public.

The small town of Peterborough is the home of America's oldest public library, which was founded in 1833. New Hampshire has a strong statewide library system. Colleges such as Dartmouth and Keene State College also feature extensive libraries for use by scholars.

▼ Yankee Publishing is New Hampshire's largest publisher, producing its namesake magazine as well as the world-famous *The Old Farmer's Almanac.*

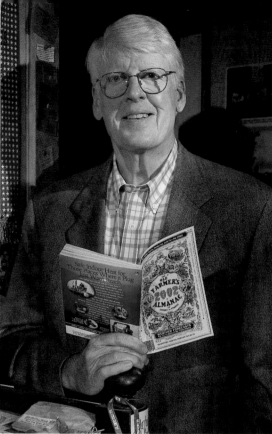

▶ Jud Hale, editor-in-chief of *The Old Farmer's Almanac*, stands in his office in Dublin with the 2002 edition of North America's oldest continuously published periodical. The Almanac was first published in 1792 during George Washington's second term as president.

Communications

New Hampshire has seven daily newspapers. The largest is the *Union Leader*, which is published in Manchester. New Hampshire also has a number of regional newspapers that are published weekly or monthly.

Several magazines are published in New Hampshire. The most well known is *Yankee*, a magazine dedicated to life in New England. The Yankee Publishing Company in Dublin has been in business since 1935. In addition to *Yankee*, which has a paid circulation of about five hundred thousand subscribers, Yankee Publishing also publishes several travel guides and *The Old Farmer's Almanac*. Several regional magazines, such as *Northern New Hampshire* and *Valley Fun,* are also published in the state. A medical magazine called *Healthcare Review* is published in Nashua, and *Unravel the Gavel*, a magazine aimed at people who attend auctions, is published in Belmont.

Five television stations serve New Hampshire. Three of these are public broadcasting stations: WENH in Durham, WEKW in Keene, and WLED in Littleton. WNDS in Derry is an independent station. The state's only network station is WMUR, an ABC affiliate in Manchester. New Hampshire residents also receive broadcasts from neighboring cities, such as Boston, Massachusetts, and Burlington, Vermont.

Music and Theater

Although it is small, New Hampshire has a thriving music and theater scene. The Colonial Theater in Keene has been putting on performances for more than seventy-five years. Its building hosts many different events, including plays, concerts, operas, and classic movies.

Peterborough has been called "the city of the arts." Only six thousand people live in this village, home to the Monadnock Music Chamber Orchestra, a theater group

called the Peterborough Players, and a children's puppet group known as the New England Marionettes. Peterborough is also proud of the MacDowell Colony, an artist's colony that provides a peaceful retreat for writers, painters, and musicians. Every year, the MacDowell Award is given to an outstanding artist, writer, composer, architect, or filmmaker. Playwright Thornton Wilder and composer Aaron Copland are just a few of the famous people who have come to the MacDowell Colony.

Sports

New Hampshire does not have any professional major league teams, but residents are still very interested in sports. New Hampshirites support the athletic teams of their local colleges, especially those of Dartmouth College and the University of New Hampshire.

Residents make full use of the state's sporting opportunities, especially outdoors. Skiing and snowboarding are extremely popular, along with hiking, boating, swimming, and mountain climbing.

New Hampshire residents also enjoy motor sports. A three-hundred-lap auto race is held in Loudon every July. Laconia is the site of Motorcycle Week, a series of races held at the New Hampshire Speedway every year that attracts more than one hundred thousand visitors.

New Hampshire Greats

Carlton Fisk was born in Vermont in 1947, but he grew up in Charlestown, New Hampshire. Fisk played with the Boston Red Sox and the Chicago White Sox. His most celebrated home run was for the Red Sox in the twelfth inning of Game Six of the 1975 World Series. The catcher was inducted into the National Baseball Hall of Fame in 2000.

▶ Carlton Fisk shows off his plaque and celebrates his induction into the National Baseball Hall of Fame, Sunday, July 23, 2000 in Cooperstown, New York. Tony Perez and Sparky Anderson were also inducted on the same day.

Great New Hampshirites

Nearly half of my poems must actually have been written in New Hampshire. . . . Four of my children were born in Derry, New Hampshire. . . . So you see it has been New Hampshire with me all the way. You will find my poems show it, I think.

— *Poet Robert Frost, 1938*

Following are only a few of the thousands of people who were born, died, or spent much of their lives in New Hampshire and made extraordinary contributions to the state and the nation.

DANIEL WEBSTER
LAWYER AND PUBLIC OFFICAL

BORN: *January 18, 1782, Salisbury (now Franklin)*
DIED: *October 24, 1852, Marshfield, MA*

Daniel Webster has been called "New Hampshire's greatest native son." Webster served in the U.S. House of Representatives and the Senate, and he was also the U.S. secretary of state under three presidents. A dynamic public speaker, Webster was also famous for his abilities as a lawyer. In "The Devil and Daniel Webster," a famous short story by Stephen Vincent Benét, Webster even beats the Devil himself in a legal battle for the soul of a New Hampshire farmer. Despite his fame and abilities, Webster was never able to achieve his greatest dream of becoming president. Although he opposed slavery, Webster was willing to compromise with the South on the issue because he felt that keeping the United States whole was more important. This commitment to unity led to his loss of the Whig party's presidential nomination in 1836.

SARAH JOSEPHA HALE
EDITOR AND AUTHOR

BORN: *October 24, 1788, Newport*
DIED: *April 30, 1879, Philadelphia, PA*

Sarah Josepha Buell Hale was a woman of many talents. In 1828, she became the first female magazine editor in the United States when she was named editor of *Ladies' Magazine*, which was later renamed *Godey's Lady's Book*. This magazine was the most popular and influential women's magazine of its day. Hale also wrote extensively for the magazine. Perhaps her best-known work was "Mary Had a Little Lamb," which she wrote in 1830. For thirty-five years, Hale worked to make Thanksgiving a national holiday. Finally, in 1863, she persuaded President Abraham Lincoln to make the day official.

SALMON P. CHASE
U.S. SUPREME COURT JUSTICE

BORN: *January 13, 1808, Cornish*
DIED: *May 7, 1873, New York, NY*

Salmon Portland Chase was the ninth of eleven children. After graduating from Dartmouth College, he worked as a lawyer in Cincinnati, creating the Statutes of Ohio, a definitive reference work for the state's judicial system. Chase was a fierce opponent of slavery. He defended so many runaway slaves that he was called "the Attorney General of Fugitive Slaves." He held office as Ohio's governor, served in the U.S. Senate, and became secretary of the treasury under Abraham Lincoln. He created a national banking system and issued the first green dollar bills. In 1864, Lincoln appointed Chase as chief justice of the Supreme Court. In 1868, Chase presided over the impeachment trial of President Andrew Johnson. Chase's great ambition was to be president, but he was never selected to run because of his controversial opinion that black men should have the right to vote. Chase remained active in politics and public affairs until his death. Today, his picture appears on the $10,000 bill.

HORACE GREELEY
JOURNALIST AND POLITICAL LEADER

BORN: *February 3, 1811, Amherst*
DIED: *November 29, 1872, New York, NY*

Called "the best newspaper editor of his time," Horace Greeley was the founder and editor of the *New York Tribune*. Greeley wrote many powerful editorials, protesting slavery, stressing the importance of public education, and encouraging citizens to understand and utilize their constitutional rights. In 1867, Greeley published a column that advised young people, who were struggling to find work in New York City, to "Go west, young man." Millions of people listened, heading west to transform the nation. Greeley also had a thriving political career. He was a delegate to the 1860 Republican Party's national convention where he helped Abraham Lincoln win the nomination for president. He later broke ties with the Republican Party and, in 1872, was the Democratic Party's presidential nominee, running against Ulysses S. Grant. Greeley lost the election and although he died less than a month later, he is still remembered today.

MARY BAKER EDDY
RELIGIOUS LEADER

BORN:: *July 16, 1821, Bow*
DIED: *December 3, 1910, Chestnut Hill, MA*

Mary Baker Eddy spent most of her life in New Hampshire, but her fame spread all over the world. In 1866, she suffered a severe fall. During her long recovery, she turned to the Bible. Her studies led her

to create a system of spiritual healing that eventually became a religion called Christian Science. She also wrote a popular book called *Science and Health with Key to the Scriptures* (1875). In 1908, Eddy founded *The Christian Science Monitor,* which is still one of the most respected newspapers in the world.

DANIEL CHESTER FRENCH
SCULPTOR

BORN: *April 20, 1850, Exeter*
DIED: *October 7, 1931, Stockbridge, MA*

It seems fitting that one of the nation's most renowned sculptors was born and lived in the Granite State. Daniel Chester French's first public work was the famous statue *The Minute Man* (1875), which stands in Concord, Massachusetts, to commemorate an early battle in the American Revolution. Millions of visitors to Washington, D.C., have admired French's most famous work, the marble statue of Abraham Lincoln in the Lincoln Memorial. This awe-inspiring sculpture took from 1911 to 1922 to complete. Creating the statue took only five years, but French worked

for another six years to change Lincoln's face and the lighting before he was satisfied that the president looked dignified.

ROBERT FROST
POET

BORN: *March 26, 1874, San Francisco, CA*
DIED: *January 29, 1963, Boston, MA*

Robert Frost was one of the nation's leading poets. He won four Pulitzer Prizes for his work and became famous around the world. Although he was born in California, his family moved to Derry when he was eleven years old. Frost briefly attended Dartmouth College and spent many years in Derry and Franconia, where he farmed, wrote, and raised his family. Many of Frost's poems, including "Mending Wall" and "Stopping by Woods on a Snowy Evening," celebrate the simple life of rural New Hampshire; in 1923, he published a book of poems titled *New Hampshire*. One of his last public appearances was at President John F. Kennedy's inauguration in 1961, when he moved the crowd by reading an original poem about the new president.

J. D. SALINGER
AUTHOR
BORN: *January 1, 1919, New York, NY*

Author J. D. (Jerome David) Salinger became one of the nation's most famous authors when he published *The Catcher in the Rye* in 1951. This novel about a teenage boy struggling to make sense of life spoke to a generation of young people and is still required reading for many high school students today. Salinger also wrote the popular novel *Franny and Zooey (1961),* as well as many short stories. Salinger has not published a new work in many years. He lives quietly in Cornish where his eccentric and reclusive ways have made him a mysterious and fascinating figure in the literary world.

ALAN SHEPARD
ASTRONAUT

BORN: *November 18, 1923, East Derry*
DIED: *July 21, 1998, Monterey, CA*

As a child, Alan Bartlett Shepard, Jr. — the man who would become the first American in space — was fascinated by Charles Lindbergh, the first man to fly solo across the Atlantic Ocean. Shepard pursued a career in the armed forces. He graduated from the U.S. Naval Academy and later attended U.S. Navy Test Pilot School and the Naval War College. In 1959, Shepard was selected as one of America's first seven astronauts. On May 5, 1961, his *Freedom 7* capsule rocketed 117 miles above the Earth on a fifteen-minute flight. In 1963, while preparing for another space flight, Shepard suffered an inner ear disorder that affected his balance and hearing. The condition kept him from flying until he had surgery a few years later. In 1971, Shepard commanded *Apollo 14*'s nine-day flight to the Moon, becoming the fifth man to walk on the lunar surface. Shepard retired in 1974 and became a successful businessman until his death from leukemia in 1998.

DAVID SOUTER
U.S. SUPREME COURT JUSTICE

BORN: *September 17, 1939, Melrose, MA*

Although Souter's family lived in Massachusetts, he spent most of his childhood in Weare. After his grandparents died, eleven-year-old David Hackett Souter and his parents moved to Weare permanently. Souter studied law at Harvard University and was a Rhodes Scholar at Oxford University. Returning to New Hampshire, he accepted a position with a Concord law firm. He later became a judge and the attorney general of New Hampshire. In 1983, the governor appointed Souter to the New Hampshire Supreme Court. In 1990, President George Bush named Souter to the U.S. Supreme Court. He is known as the court's intellectual leader.

ADAM SANDLER
ACTOR AND COMEDIAN

BORN: *September 9, 1966, Brooklyn, NY*

Adam Sandler grew up in Manchester, where he had a reputation as the class clown. His first professional appearance was at a Boston comedy club when he was seventeen years old. During college, he appeared on the popular TV show *The Cosby Show*. Shortly after graduating with a bachelor of fine arts degree from New York University in New York City, he began writing and performing on *Saturday Night Live*. He made several comedy albums and had a hit record with "Hanukkah Song," a funny holiday song that celebrates his Jewish heritage. Sandler went on to star in *Happy Gilmore, The Wedding Singer, The Waterboy, Big Daddy, Mr. Deeds,* and the critically acclaimed *Punch-Drunk Love*. Sandler's goofy charm has made him a popular celebrity.

New Hampshire
History At-A-Glance

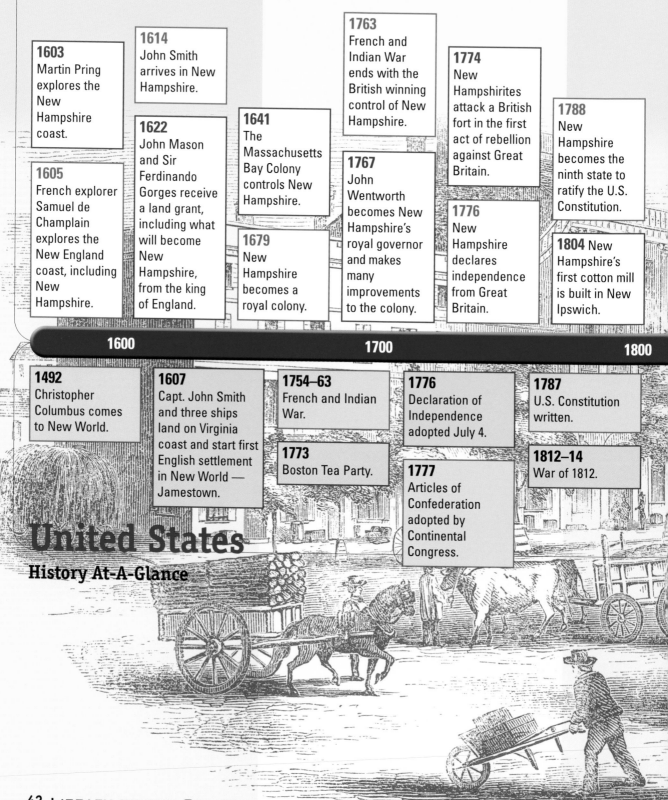

1603
Martin Pring explores the New Hampshire coast.

1605
French explorer Samuel de Champlain explores the New England coast, including New Hampshire.

1614
John Smith arrives in New Hampshire.

1622
John Mason and Sir Ferdinando Gorges receive a land grant, including what will become New Hampshire, from the king of England.

1641
The Massachusetts Bay Colony controls New Hampshire.

1679
New Hampshire becomes a royal colony.

1763
French and Indian War ends with the British winning control of New Hampshire.

1767
John Wentworth becomes New Hampshire's royal governor and makes many improvements to the colony.

1774
New Hampshirites attack a British fort in the first act of rebellion against Great Britain.

1776
New Hampshire declares independence from Great Britain.

1788
New Hampshire becomes the ninth state to ratify the U.S. Constitution.

1804 New Hampshire's first cotton mill is built in New Ipswich.

1600   **1700**   **1800**

1492
Christopher Columbus comes to New World.

1607
Capt. John Smith and three ships land on Virginia coast and start first English settlement in New World — Jamestown.

1754–63
French and Indian War.

1773
Boston Tea Party.

1776
Declaration of Independence adopted July 4.

1777
Articles of Confederation adopted by Continental Congress.

1787
U.S. Constitution written.

1812–14
War of 1812.

United States
History At-A-Glance

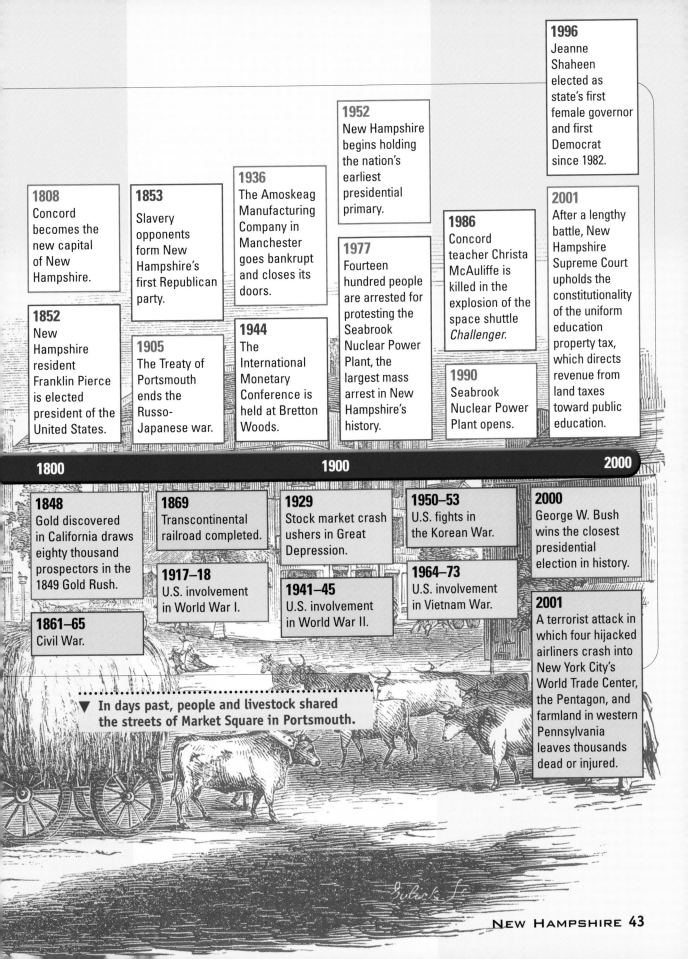

1996
Jeanne Shaheen elected as state's first female governor and first Democrat since 1982.

1952
New Hampshire begins holding the nation's earliest presidential primary.

1936
The Amoskeag Manufacturing Company in Manchester goes bankrupt and closes its doors.

1808
Concord becomes the new capital of New Hampshire.

1853
Slavery opponents form New Hampshire's first Republican party.

1986
Concord teacher Christa McAuliffe is killed in the explosion of the space shuttle *Challenger.*

2001
After a lengthy battle, New Hampshire Supreme Court upholds the constitutionality of the uniform education property tax, which directs revenue from land taxes toward public education.

1852
New Hampshire resident Franklin Pierce is elected president of the United States.

1905
The Treaty of Portsmouth ends the Russo-Japanese war.

1944
The International Monetary Conference is held at Bretton Woods.

1977
Fourteen hundred people are arrested for protesting the Seabrook Nuclear Power Plant, the largest mass arrest in New Hampshire's history.

1990
Seabrook Nuclear Power Plant opens.

1800   **1900**   **2000**

1848
Gold discovered in California draws eighty thousand prospectors in the 1849 Gold Rush.

1869
Transcontinental railroad completed.

1929
Stock market crash ushers in Great Depression.

1950–53
U.S. fights in the Korean War.

2000
George W. Bush wins the closest presidential election in history.

1917–18
U.S. involvement in World War I.

1941–45
U.S. involvement in World War II.

1964–73
U.S. involvement in Vietnam War.

1861–65
Civil War.

2001
A terrorist attack in which four hijacked airliners crash into New York City's World Trade Center, the Pentagon, and farmland in western Pennsylvania leaves thousands dead or injured.

▼ In days past, people and livestock shared the streets of Market Square in Portsmouth.

Festivals and Fun for All

Check web site for exact date and directions.

Candlelight Stroll at Strawbery Banke, **Portsmouth**

Every year, the Strawbery Banke Museum holds a special evening tour of the buildings and grounds. Explore the houses, gardens, and other attractions by candlelight on this guided tour.
www.strawberybanke.org

Children's Day, **Portsmouth**

This celebration is full of family fun. Children and adults alike can enjoy steamship rides, a bicycle rodeo, a petting zoo, craft demonstrations, contests, magicians, and music.
www.proportsmouth.org/cday

Chowderfest, **Portsmouth**

Seafood chowder is a traditional food of New Hampshire's coastal communities. Taste the many different varieties of this tasty soup at this festival of food and fun.
www.portcity.org/funLeisure.cfm

First Night, **Portsmouth, Wolfeboro, and other communities**

Every New Year's Eve, several New Hampshire towns hold family-friendly festivals. Travel the streets and enjoy face painting, ice sculpture contests, food, concerts, and fireworks.
www.proportsmouth.org/firstnight
www.wolfeboroonline.com/firstnight/index.html

Freedom Old Home Week, **Freedom**

This weeklong celebration includes music, parades, craft fairs, sports tournaments, and plenty of home-style cooking.
www.ossipeevalley.org/freedom.htm

Hampton Beach Seafood Festival, **Hampton Beach**

Taste the bounty of the sea as more than fifty restaurants prepare seafood dishes for people to try. The festival also includes a craft fair and different types of entertainment.
www.hamptonbeach.org/calendar/

Hillsboro Balloon Festival, **Hillsboro**

Every summer, the skies over Hillsboro come alive with dozens of hot-air balloons. The festival also includes an antique and classic car show, a parade, and truck and tractor pulls.
www.balloonfestival.org

Hopkinton State Fair, **Contoocook**

This old-fashioned country fair features many agricultural events, a petting zoo, live entertainment, and a midway of

exciting rides. Visitors can also tour a museum of farming memorabilia.
www.hsfair.org

Market Square Day, **Portsmouth**

Stroll the streets of Portsmouth and enjoy arts and crafts, food, shopping, and entertainment during this summertime festival.
www.portcity.org/ funLeisure.com

New Hampshire Highland Games, **Contoocook**

The Highland Games are one of the largest Scottish festivals in the northeast. Visitors can enjoy traditional Scottish music and athletics, watch the gathering of the clans, and attend sheepdog herding trials.
www.nhscot.org

Pemi Valley Annual Bluegrass Festival, **Campton**

Enjoy traditional music at this outdoor festival, which also includes family games and activities and plenty of food.
www.pemivalleybluegrass.com

Prescott Park Arts Festival, **Portsmouth**

Beautiful Prescott Park is the site of this annual event, which includes dance, theater, and musical performances by a variety of New Hampshire artists.
www.artfest.org

▶ A dog sled speeds across the New Hampshire countryside. The New England Sled Dog Club was organized in New Hampshire in 1924.

Riverfest Celebration, **Manchester**

From musicians to clowns, fireworks to contests, this celebration along the waterfront is a popular family event.
www.manchester-chamber.org/ visitors/culture-rec.asp

Rochester Fair, **Rochester**

This old-fashioned country fair includes harness racing, horse shows, clowns, carnival rides, musical performances, and a demolition derby.
www.rochesterfair.com

Stark Fiddler's Contest, **Stark**

Enjoy down-home music and family fun at this annual musical event.
www.windhill.com/stark

Warner Fall Foliage Festival, **Warner**

Every fall, visitors can admire the beauty of New Hampshire's foliage while enjoying a country fair that includes a road race, oxen pulls, a parade, carnival rides, and a traditional pie-eating contest.
www.wfff.org

World Championship Sled Dog Racing Derby, **Laconia**

This event, which has been held for more than seventy years, features an exciting sled dog race through the streets of Laconia.
www.weirsonline.com/winter.htm

Books

Banks, Kate. *Dillon Dillon*. New York: Farrar, Straus and Giroux, 2002. A boy's relationship with three loons on a lake near his New Hampshire cabin helps him make sense of his own life.

Blos, Joan W. *A Gathering of Days: A New England Girl's Journal, 1830–32*. New York: Atheneum, 1979. A fictionalized account of growing up in New Hampshire during the early 1830s. Winner of the 1980 Newbery Medal.

Bober, Natalie S. *A Restless Spirit: The Story of Robert Frost*. New York: Henry Holt, 1998. A biography of Robert Frost, one of New Hampshire's most famous residents.

Casanave, Suki. *Natural Wonders of New Hampshire: A Guide to Parks, Preserves and Wild Places*. Castine, Maine: Country Roads Press, 1994. A guide to the natural forests and other scenic places in New Hampshire.

Fradin, Dennis Brindell. *The New Hampshire Colony*. Chicago: Children's Press, 1992. A detailed account of New Hampshire's early history.

Marsh, Carole. *New Hampshire History! Surprising Secrets About Our State's Founding Mothers, Fathers & Kids!* Atlanta: Gallopede Publishing Group, 1996. A lively and entertaining look at New Hampshire's history and famous people.

Otfinoski, Steven. *Celebrate the States: New Hampshire*. Tarrytown, NY: Benchmark Books, 1999. An overview of New Hampshire's geography, history, and politics, with interesting first-person accounts from natives.

Shannon, Terry Miller. *From Sea to Shining Sea: New Hampshire*. New York: Children's Press, 2002. A brief look at New Hampshire, illustrated with many captivating photographs.

Web Sites

▶ New Hampshire State Government Online
www.state.nh.us

▶ New Hampshire Division of Travel and Tourism Development
www.visitnh.gov

▶ New Hampshire State Library
webster.state.nh.us/nhsl

▶ New Hampshire Historical Society
www.nhhistory.org